Arm Knitting Tutorial Book

Knitting Guideline With Simple Pattern To Try

Copyright © 2023

DEDICATION

Contents

Misty Goddess Arm Knit Wrap 1

15 Minute Vest 3

One Point Wrap 7

Eggplant and Orchid Cowl 9

Princess Scarf 15

Oversized Arm Knit Blanket 19

Arm Knit Pillow DIY 21

The Triplet Shawl 25

Stylish Scarf 28

Arm Knit Necklaces 39

Arm Knitted Wreath 42

Misty Goddess Arm Knit Wrap

Yarn Weight(6) Super Bulky/Super Chunky (4-11 stitches for 4 inches)

Gauge1 stitches, 2 rows, 3 inches. stockinette stitch

MATERIALS:

Bernat® Blissful™ (3.5 oz/100 g; 106 yds/97 m) Contrast A: Midnight Mist (89004) - 3 balls

Bernat® Blissful™ (3.5 oz/100 g; 106 yds/97 m) Contrast B: Inky Teal (89007) - 1 ball

Measurements: Approximately 18" [45.5 cm] wide x 72" [183 cm] long (excluding fringe).

INSTRUCTIONS

Note: For ease of working, wind 3 balls of A and 1 ball of B into 1 ball before beginning.

Holding 3 strands of A and 1 strand of B together, cast on 11 stitches.

Arm knit until work measures approximately 72" [183 cm], noting right side is facing you.

Cast off.

Fringe: Cut strands of A and B 20" [51 cm] long.

Taking 3 strands of A and 1 strand of B together, fold in half and knot into 8 fringes evenly spaced across each end of Wrap. Trim fringe evenly.

15 Minute Vest

Yarn Weight(6) Super Bulky/Super Chunky (4-11 stitches for 4 inches)

MATERIALS:

Rozetti Yarns Charade (75% acrylic, 7% metallic, 18% polyamide;

100g/13 yds)

620-12 Heliotrope (MC) – 2 (3, 4) skeins

620-04 Amber Waves (CC) – 1 (2, 2) skeins

Needles: Your arms!

Notions: Tapestry needle, sewing needle and thread

GAUGE

Varies from arm to arm!

Gauge achieved in sample in for which finished measurements are based:

1.75 sts x 2 rows = 4"

SIZES

Extra Small/Small (Medium/Large, 1X/2X)

Shown in Small size

FINISHED MEASUREMENTS

Back Width: 16 (20, 24)"

Height: 10½ (12¼, 12¼)"

NOTES

This vest is worked by knitting with your arms. Knit as you would normally knit, except use your arms instead of knitting needles!

When changing colors, use the intarsia method, twisting the strands together to prevent holes from forming in your work.

INSTRUCTIONS

VEST

With MC, cast on 6 (7, 7) sts to your left arm.

 Front

Row 1: With MC, knit.

Row 2: With MC k4 (5, 5), with CC k2.

Row 3: With CC k2, with MC k4 (5, 5).

Rows 4 & 5: Rep Rows 2 & 3.

Row 6 (Armhole row): With MC k2 (3, 3), k2tog, yo, with CC k2.

Rep Rows 2 & 3, 0 (1, 2) more times.

 Back

Row 1: With CC k2, with MC k4 (5, 5).

Row 2: With MC k4 (5, 5), with CC k2.

Rows 3-8 (10, 12): Rep Rows 1 & 2.

 Front

Row 1 (Armhole row): With CC k2, with MC yo, k2 (3, 3)

Row 2: With MC k4 (5, 5), with CC k2.

Row 3: With CC k2, with MC k4 (5, 5).

Rows 4 & 5: Rep Rows 2 & 3.

Rep Rows 2 & 3, 0 (1, 2) more times.

Next row: With MC, knit. Bind off all sts using MC.

 FINISHING

Secure ends with sewing needle and thread.

To wear, put your arms through the holes

One Point Wrap

Yarn Weight(6) Super Bulky/Super Chunky (4-11 stitches for 4 inches)

APPROXIMATE LENGTH:

46" (117cm), to point

STRANDS:

Use 5 strands held together throughout

MATERIALS:

5 skeins super bulky weight yarn, 1 color

3 ceramic buttons (1 1/2" [4cm])

Alternative Closure

Don't feel like sewing on buttons? Use a pretty jewelry piece or a decorative shawl stick as a closure instead.

INSTRUCTIONS

Wrap

Using 5 strands held together, cast on 7 stitches.

Work in Plain Stitch for 15 rows.

DECREASE SECTION

Row 1: Decrease 1 at start of row as shown on page 14.

Row 2: Decrease 1 at end of row.

Rows 3–6: Repeat Rows 1–2 once, then repeat Row 1 once more.

Row 7: Work last 2 stitches together, acting as both a decrease and a bind-off.

Finishing

Arrange buttons on flat edge of wrap as shown in photo and sew on using a strand of yarn.

Weave in all ends.

Eggplant and Orchid Cowl

MATERIALS:

3 Skeins of your favorite super bulky weight yarn. Yarn shown in project is Lion Brand's Homespun in "Baroque" and "Barrington" and Wool Ease Thick & Quick in "Denim" (I used about 1/2 of each skein)

1 large button (button shown is two inches wide)

Large tapestry needle

Scissors

Your arms!

Note: You can use any bulky/super bulky yarns for this project, if you are unsure about your yarn and/or the colors you have chosen, you can do a test swatch to see how everything will come together.

Sizing:

Approximately 10 inches tall

Approximately 40 inches wide

Note: Measurements were taken with garment laying flat on a table and not stretched out.

To wear it a a long cowl/infinity scarf, wear it with the button at the nape of the neck and let the front hang down low.

INSTRUCTIONS

Cast on 24 stitches.

Row 1: Knit all stitches.

Repeat row 1 for a total of 4 rows.

Bind off all stitches.

Finishing & Assembly:

With wrong side (purl ridges) facing, fold sides inward and determine button placement. Sew button to upper corner of piece with a matching piece of yarn. Weave in any ends that remain.

Princess Scarf

Yarn Weight(6) Super Bulky/Super Chunky (4-11 stitches for 4 inches)

Gauge1 stitches, 2 rows, 3 inches. stockinette stitch

MATERIALS:

Red Heart® Grande™ 565 Orchid - 1 ball

Measurements: Circumference is approximately 45" (114 cm), depending on size of stitches.

Gauge: Gauge is not important for this project.

INSTRUCTIONS

SCARF

Make a large slip knot 3 yards from the end of the ball. Slide it onto your right arm.

Cast On Row: Hold the working yarn (from the ball) and the tail in your left hand as if doing a regular long-tail cast-on. The tail is in front (around your thumb) and the working yarn is in the back (around your index finger).

Move your right hand under the front strand, pick up loop on finger and pull through loop on thumb, place on right arm.

Repeat 10 more times until you have 12 cast on stitches on right arm, making sure that they are not too snug on your arm.

Row 1: Hold the working yarn in your right hand. With your left hand, pull the stitch at your right wrist off of your right hand. Take the loop now in your right hand and put it on your left arm. You have now knit your first stitch.

Repeat for all stitches on your right arm so your left arm has 12 stitches and your right arm has none.

Row 2: Hold the working yarn in your left hand. With your right hand, pull the stitch at your left wrist off of your left hand. Take the loop now in your left hand and put it on your right arm. Repeat for all stitches on your left arm so your right arm has 12 stitches and your left arm has none.

Repeat Rows 1 and 2 until piece is about 45" (114 cm) long and you have at least 3 yards of yarn left for bind off and to sew the ends together.

Bind Off Row: Knit the first two stitches of the row as in previous rows. Drop the yarn from your hand, and pull the first stitch over the second stitch and off of your hand. You now have one stitch left on your arm. Knit another stitch, drop the yarn, and pull the second stitch over the third stitch and off of your hand. Continue in this manner until the row is complete and there is one stitch left on your arm. Cut the end from the ball leaving enough yarn to sew ends together. Pull the tail through the final stitch and knot to secure.

FINISHING

To keep the ends from coming undone, knot each end around the nearest stitch of the scarf. Use the tails to sew the ends of the scarf together, knot and then cut the excess.

Oversized Arm Knit Blanket

MATERIALS:

11 Skeins of Couture Jazz yarn in slate

INSTRUCTIONS

Cast on 27 stitches

Arm knit until you have used 10 1/2 skeins

Bind off loosely to keep from making a skinnier edge

Weave in your ends

19

To attach each new skein, tie a double knot and trim the excess to the shape of the knot.

Keep your stitches as tight as possible by keeping them at the smallest part of your arm and making sure the stitches aren't twisted. If the stitches are twisted they will be unable to tighten all the way.

Arm Knit Pillow DIY

MATERIALS:

2 Skeins of T Shirt Yarn (or sweatshirt yarn, my new fave). I handmade mine, but you can find it for sale at Walmart.

Arm Knitting Tutorial, found HERE.

Pillow Insert

Darning Needle (Optional)

INSTRUCTIONS

Arm knit 2 squares, about the same size as your pillow insert. I was using very thick yarn, and was able to do this with 10 stitches. Keep a very long tail on one of your knit squares.

Place the pillow in between your two knit squares, and pin together in various places around the side edges. Slip a darning needle on the end of your tail.

Go back and forth with the needle through the stitches around the side edges of your pillow, securing the two knit squares together all the way around. When finished, simply cut the tail with about 5 – 10"

remaining, and weave it through the pillow to hide the loose end.

In all fairness, you can probably do something way fancier here – like the mattress stitch Anne talks about at Flax & Twine. I was just keeping it simple. Weave that bad boy together any old way you want – so long as one side sticks to the other – and the pillow is held firmly in place in the middle!

The Triplet Shawl

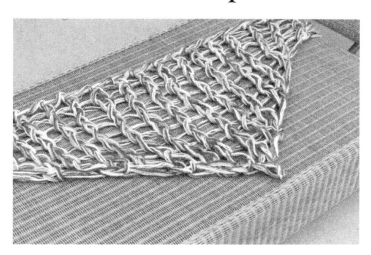

MATERIALS:

5 skeins of worsted weight yarn in complimentary colors

Your arms

Scissors

INSTRUCTIONS

Cast on 28 stitches, using all 5 strands of yarn together as if they were 1 strand.

Row 1: knit

Row 2: knit 2 together, knit until there are two stitches left, knit 2 together

Repeat row 2 for the next 11 rows until there are only 4 stitches remaining.

Row 13: knit 2 together, knit 2 together

Bind off the remaining 2 stitches

Weave in the ends and try on your new shawl!

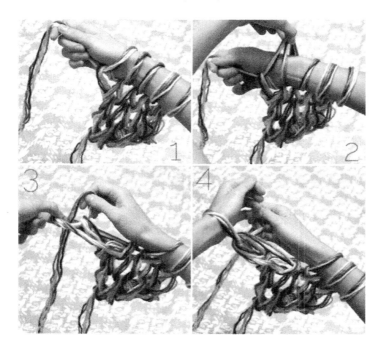

You can throw it over your shoulders to wear it as a shawl, wrap it around your waist to use it as a swimsuit cover-up, or fold it in half and tie it at the back of your neck to create a bandana scarf.

Stylish Scarf

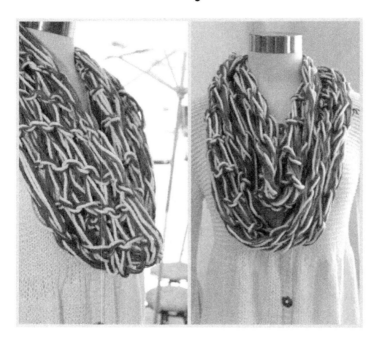

INSTRUCTIONS (and make this scarf)

Make a slip knot with a long tail and put over your right arm. Tighten, but keep it a bit loose so it is easy to slide on your arm.

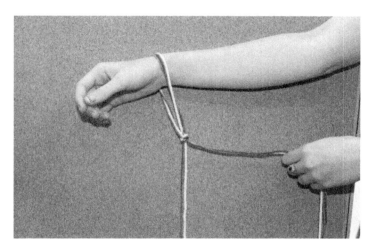

You will now cast on stitches in the same way you would long tail cast stitches onto a needle. Pretend your arm is the needle in this instance.

If you need more help casting on, watch this video and envision your arm as the needle. The video is a bit easier to see than these pictures.

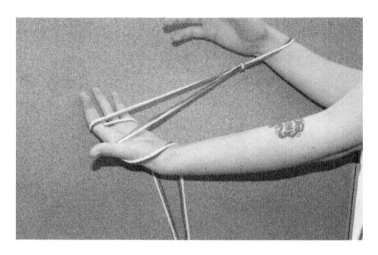

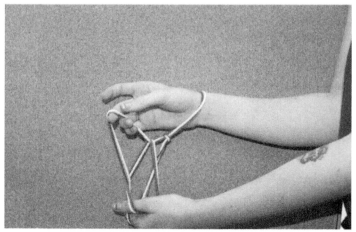

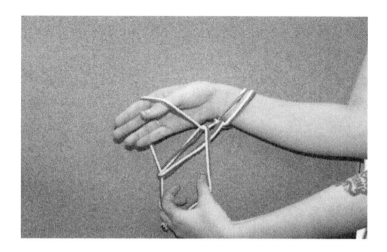

Cast on Ten stitches

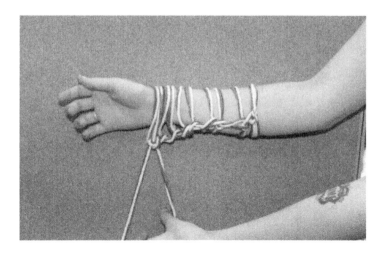

Ten stitches cast onto your arm.

To knit your first stitch, hold the yarn that is attached to your ball in your right hand (the arm that has all of the stitches on it)

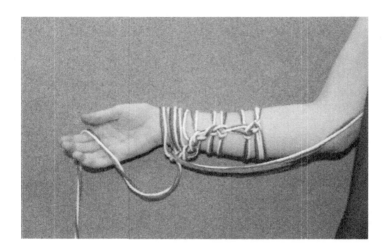

Grab the yarn with your right hand and pull the first stitch on your arm over your hand while pulling the yarn you are holding through the stitch.

This will make what looks like a loop.

Now put your left hand through this loop and tighten the stitch onto your left arm by pulling the working yarn.

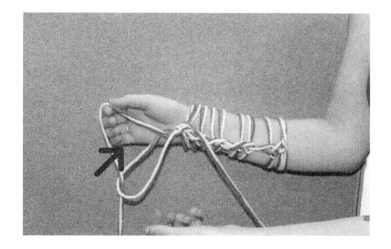

The arrow indicates the loop to put your hand through

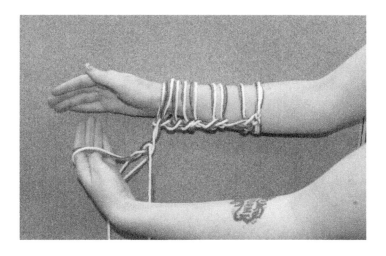

Hold the yarn in your right hand again, and repeat the process. Grab the yarn with your right hand and pull the next stitch on your right arm over your right hand.

Put the loop you've just formed over your left hand and tighten onto your left arm.

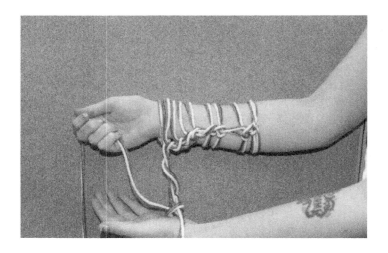

Hold working yarn in hand

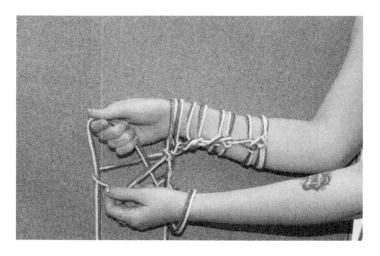

Pull stitch on your arm over your hand

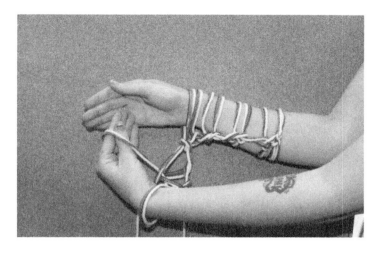

Place loop/stitch that is formed onto your left hand

Continue this with the rest of the stitches until they are all on your left arm. You have just arm knitted one row!

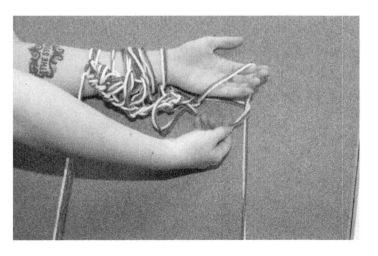

Knitted one row, now onto the second

Now reverse the process. Hold the working yarn in your LEFT hand and pull the stitch over, forming the loop that you place your right hand through.

Continue to do this until the end of the row.

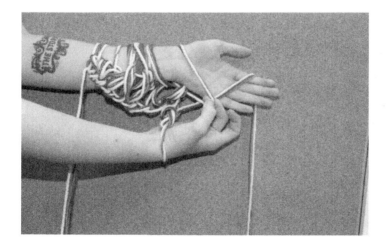

Knit as many rows as you want to obtain the correct length for your scarf. We continued until the scarf would wrap around your neck twice, but it can be made shorter or longer, depending on the look you want! It is easy to judge the length as you go and adjust the length.

Once your piece starts to make progress...

Bind off the same way you would on needles. Knit two stitches and then pull the first stitch you made over the second stitch and off of your hand. Knit another stitch (so there are two on the your arm again) and pull the previous stitch over the new stitch and your hand. Watch this video if you need more help binding off.

Once you've bound off, take the cast on edge and bind off edge of your arm scarf and place them together. Seam them together by weaving yarn into each stitch across the row loosely and tying off at end.

37

Voila! An arm-knitted scarf. You can do this with chunkier yarn or with more stitches to make rugs or blankets with a tighter weave. This scarf wraps around your neck twice, but it can be made shorter or longer, depending on the look you want!

Arm Knit Necklaces

MATERIALS:

Bernat Softee Chunky, in color: Soft Taupe

Bernat Sheep(ish) by Vickie Howell, in color: Hot Pink(ish), Coral(ish) OR Turquoise(ish)

Bernat Roving, in color: Rice Paper

Bernat Soft Boucle, in color: White

2, Macrame Beades

Very Large Eyed Yarn Needle

Spray Primer & Metallic Paint (optional)

2, Jewlelry O-rings

1, Necklace Clasp

Jewelry Wire

Jewelry Pliers

SPECIAL ABBREVIATION

AK = arm knit

GAUGE Doesn't matter — woohoo!

INSTRUCTIONS

Holding all four strands of yarn together as if they were one yarn and leaving at least a 10"/25cm tail, cast on 3 sts.

1st Row: AK to end.

2nd Row: Slip all sts back onto the arm you just knit them off of; the working yarn will now be at the end of the row (closest to your elbow), instead of the beginning.

Bring the working yarn behind your work and AK the 1st stitch (the one closest to your wrist); AK to end. This method creates i-cord.

Repeat 2nd Row until piece measures 12"/30.5 cm.

BO, leaving at least at least a 10"/25cm tail

FINISHING

Prime and spray paint macrame beads; let dry.

Using a large-eyed yarn needle, feed tail strands through macrame bead; tie a knot to secure. Repeat on opposite side.

Braid tail strands (optional).

Using Jewelry pliers, generously wrap wire around tail strands of both ends; leave small space under last wrap; smoosh with pliers to secure.

Attach o-ring through wire wrap space on both ends. Attach necklace clasp onto one o-ring.

Arm Knitted Wreath

MATERIALS:

Chunky wool (you'll need about 2 pounds) Make sure to use my code JAN10 for a 10% discount to BeCozi

1 wooden wreath frame

Anenome and rosette felt flowers (check out my felt flower DIY)

Glue gun

Sewing thread

Ribbon

INSTRUCTIONS

Make a loose knot with you single strand of yarn.

Grab the free strand of yarn and pull it through the loop and form another loop.

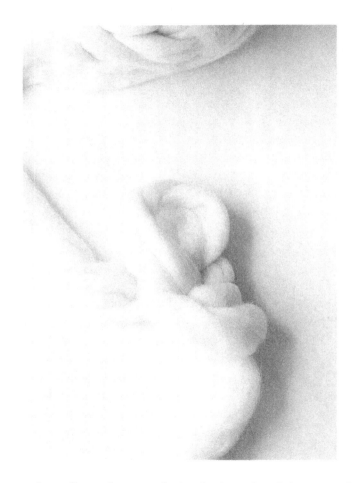

Repeat step 2 until you have a chain the length of the wreath.

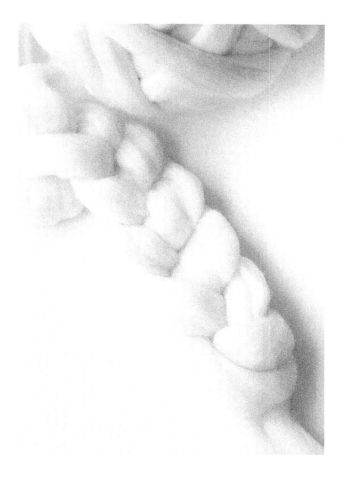

Place your arm knitted chain on top of the wreath and secure it with your glue gun.

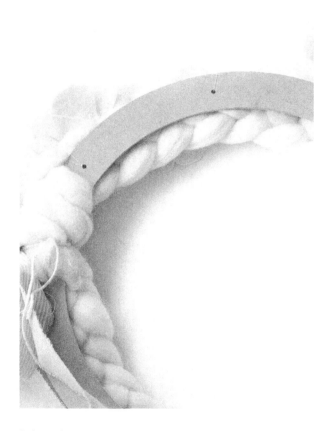

Tuck ends of the chain under the wreath.

You can also, thread through the holes and the wreath to secure it even more.

Place bow and felt flowers on your wreath with glue.

Printed in Great Britain
by Amazon